1 MONTH OF
FREE
READING

at

www.ForgottenBooks.com

By purchasing this book you are
eligible for one month membership to
ForgottenBooks.com, giving you
unlimited access to our entire
collection of over 1,000,000 titles via
our web site and mobile apps.

To claim your free month visit:

www.forgottenbooks.com/free870324

ISBN 978-0-265-58137-7
PIBN 10870324

- *orewor* -

IN THE PREPARATION OF THIS BROCHURE, an effort has been made to ave it serve a dual purpose: (1) as a souvenir program of the dedication ' the Edian D. Markham Memorial Building and the parsonage of Saint)seph A. M. E. Church; (2) to convey certain data concerning the found- ıg and progress of the African Methodist Episcopal Church.

Material has been assembled from the following sources: experiences ' members of Saint Joseph; Encyclopedia Britannica; Encyclopedia of frican Methodism, compiled by Bishop R. R. Wright, Jr.; Methodist olity by Bishop H. M. Turner; A. M. E. Discipline; Bishop Reverdy C. ansom, Director of Bureau of Research and History of the African Meth- iist Episcopal Church; and an address delivered on the History of African [ethodism, February 12, 1950, by Dr. Helen G. Edmonds, Professor of istory, North Carolina College at Durham; Journal of Negro History, ctober, 1937.

Grateful acknowledgment is herewith recorded to the Pastor, Rev. . A. Johnston, for his advice and patience; to L. E. Austin, Advertising [anager; our advertisers who helped make the publication possible; Miss vangelyn A. Vidal and Mrs. Celeste J. Smith for proofreading; Mrs. Sadie . M. Alexander, Attorney for the Philadelphia Annual Conference ıd the Bishops Council of the A. M. E. Church and Mrs. Ruth hornton, Secretary of Bethel A. M. E. Church, Philadelphia, for pictures ı connection with the early history of the A. M. E. Church; The Stanback tudios and Service Printing Company for prompt and efficient service; ıd to the membership for pictures, information and financial support ırough the purchase of copies of the brochure.

SNOW BAILEY

History of St. Joseph A. M. E. Church

The following sketch was compiled by the late Rev. J. A. Valentine, on the occasion of the Diamond Jubilee Celebration of Saint Joseph A. M. E. Church, December 10-17, 1944.

These facts were obtained from several sources, viz: my own pastoral experience, a few members who were present at its beginning and excerpts from a booklet: "Life of a Great Man, Rev. Edian D. Markham and The Founding of St. Joseph A. M. E. Church, Durham, N. C.," by William Benjamin Markham, son of the founder—Revised Edition, 1941.

Boyd's History of Durham says, "The first Negro congregation in point of time is St. Joseph African Methodist Episcopal Church. It was founded in 1869 and its first pastor was Edward Markham."

It counts among its pastors some of the most outstanding ministers of the connection, and is considered the leading A. M. E. Church in North Carolina. It includes in its membership many of the most prominent members of the

EDIAN D. MARKHAM   MOLLY MARKHAM

Freedom Certificate — Edian D. Markham

STATE OF NORTH CAROLINA.

I, Jas. W. Hinton, Clerk of the Court of Pleas and Quarter Sessions, held for the county of Pasquotank and State aforesaid, do hereby certify that the bearer hereof *Edeem Shelman* now about the age of *twenty one* years, *five* feet *two* inches high in of a *black* color, and his Stetter Early is a free person of color, he having exhibited to me (and the same is now on file,) a written certificate from *W. S. Markham* (a citizen of the County) of the free birth of him the said *Edeen Shelman* that he is a free citizen of this County and that he is therefore entitled to all the rights and privileges of Free persons of color allowed by the laws of our aforesaid State of N. Carolina.

In Testimony Whereof, I have hereunto subscribed my name, and affixed

Excerpts From Edian D. Markham's Papers

Manual of the A. M. E. Church: In the organization of the first A. M. E. Church at Durham, Rev. Edian Markham organized the first membership and bargain and bought the first ground and paid for it, August 20, 1869.

The builder of the first church, Edian Markham, hauled the first timbers. Rev. George Hunter built the first church. Rev. George Hunter hauled the first timbers.

The first bishop who had charge of the A. M. E. Churches in North Carolina was Bishop Payne, but Bishop Alexander Wayman presided in his absence.

The rise and progress of the A. M. E. Church at Durham, North Carolina, in the year 1870, August 17. I, Edian D. Markham having charge as a missionary did organize the first Methodist Church at Durham, North Carolina, which was called Durham Station at that time. From 1870 to 1900 is 30 years.

race, pioneers in business, education, and the professions.

St. Joseph Church was founded in 1869 by Rev. Edian D. Markham. Rev. Markham was born in Elizabeth City, North Carolina, April 23, 1824. He did not remember his father, but he saw his mother driven through the streets bearing chains around her ankles, to be sold to the highest bidder at the auction block, and he himself was bound and taken to Ohio.

He ran away from Ohio by way of the underground railroad into Canada, from there he went to New York where he obtained a Webster spelling book and learned to read and write. He studied the catechism and the Bible and felt that he was called to do missionary work.

In 1868 Rev. Markham came to Durham and met Mrs. Minerva Fowler, who owned a large tract of land. He purchased from her that part of the land which seemed most attractive to him and there preached and held prayer meetings. The first place that served as a church was nothing more than bushes supported by long poles which were fixed in the ground with grassy earth as its "marble floor." Under this simple bush arbor the people worshiped God. The members would sit on boxes and homemade stools as they listened to this pioneer of African Methodism.

Very soon a log church was built and from this cabin Rev. Markham preached the gospel and taught the doctrines of the African Methodist Episcopal Church.

On August 20, 1869, the church was organized with only six members. The land on which the church now stands was given by Rev. Markham. He was then called to another field, leaving the church with fifteen members. Rev. Lewis Edwards was sent to this work and was succeeded by the Rev. George Hunter, (father of Dr. A. S. Hunter, dentist and prominent member now, 1944, of St. Joseph Church). Rev. Hunter built the first frame church. After a course of time it became necessary to build a more stately structure. This was the second frame church and the following ministers helped to complete it, Reverends Hunter, Offlay, Edwards, and W. D. Cook.

The first name of the church was "Union Bethel." A little later the officers of the church planned to build a brick structure and to change its name to "St. Joseph Church." St. Joseph was commenced by Rev. Chambers. The corner stone was laid by the Masons in 1892.

This building was continued by a successive line of ministers, viz: Rev. W. J. Jordan, Rev. W. E. Walker, Rev. D. J. Beckett. St. Joseph was completed under the supervision of Rev. J. E. Jackson. It was made of brick from Robert Fitzgerald and Sons, a Negro brickyard in Durham. Booker T. Washington in commenting on St. Joseph, while

JOHN MERRICK

J. M. AVERY

visiting in Durham, said: "In all my traveling I have never seen a finer Negro church than St. Joseph."

PIONEERS

Among the pioneer members of St. Joseph Church there are many who furnished leadership both as to official positions and the handling of finances. We can name only a few: John Merrick, founder of the North Carolina Mutual Life Insurance Company, was a trustee and president of the Allen Christian Endeavor League; John M. Avery, who at his death was vice-president and secretary of North Carolina Mutual, was one of the greatest laymen in the A. M. E. Church; was delegate to seven consecutive General Conferences and a member of the General Conference Commission; Professor W. G. Pearson one of the first Negro educators of the state, as well as an outstanding pioneer in the commercial life of Durham; James Weaver, Mrs. Lillie Bullock, Mrs. Ada Thornton, George Bradshaw, Mrs. Maria Warren, Mrs. Caroline Bond, I. H. Buchanan, Mrs. Eliza Hanks, O. B. Womack, E. D. Mickle, and Dr. S. L. Warren.

Leading white citizens gave thousands of

W. G. PEARSON
Trustee

MRS. MINNIE S. PEARSON
Missionary Leader

E. D. MICKLE
Steward

Former Pastors

REV. W. C. CLELAND, D. D.

1918—1923

REV. V. C. HODGES, D. D.

1929—1936

REV. J. A. VALENTINE
S. T. B., D. D.
1936—1949

dollars to the establishment and maintenance of St. Joseph Church. Among them were: Washington Duke, General Julian Carr, W. T. Blackwell, and Mrs. Eugene Morehead.

Mrs. Molly Markham, wife of the founder was one of the first missionaries and shared with her husband in helping to make possible St. Joseph Church. She lived a long and useful Christian life. Her funeral was held at St. Joseph Church Sunday, February 23, 1941. The pastor, Rev. J. A. Valentine, in his eulogy said: "Her life is both an inspiration and a challenge, and while she is absent in the body, she will always live in memory's sacred cabinet."

Miss Maggie Markham, daughter is still living in the Markham homeplace. Benjamin Markham, son, lives with his family in Boston, Mass. Delaney Markham, grandson, and his family are active members of St. Joseph.

The following pastors have served St. Joseph Church since 1869, Reverends: E. D. Markham, Corbeal, Billy Paine, Monroe, Lewis, George Hunter, O. Ofley, Leroy Edwards, W. D. Cook, M. J. Fry, Simmons, A. J. Chambers, W. J. Jordan, L. S. Flagg, W. E. Walker, C. H. King, D. J. Beckett, J. E. Jackson, E. T. Bailey, W. R. Gullins, W. C. Cleland, L. H. Midgette, V. C. Hodges, J. A. Valentine, and D. A. Johnston.

Stewardess Board Number One — November 6, 1935

Parsonage   Edian D. Markham Memorial Building   Sanctuary

Rev. and Mrs. D. A. Johnston

The history of St. Joseph A. M. E. Church has been both interesting and glorious. Through the years this church has had some of the most outstanding ministers of our denomination as pastors. Because of the great preachers, scholars, and administrators who have pastored this church, Saint Joseph has always been regarded as one of the great churches of African Methodism. Because of the noble line of predecessors who through "blood, sweat and tears" have given unselfish service to the members of this church, the present administration salutes those stalwart Sons of the Church for their great achievements. To them we owe undying gratitude and do now confess that the achievements of the present would not have been possible without their noble efforts. In recognition of the fountainhead of any success, we thankfully acknowledge the faithful and loyal support of the membership of St. Joseph and the Hand of God that has brought us safely thus far.

THE JOHNSTONS

Rev. D. A. Johnston was assigned to Saint Joseph A. M. E. Church, November 28, 1948. He came to Durham with his heart set on the completion of the educational building. He dreamed it and preached it. After renovating the parsonage and making it comfortable for his family, he immediately set in motion plans to reach his goal. The first financial effort amounted to $5,130.58 and a second to $8,629.81. Soon there were sufficient funds to resume the work—and the educational building was completed and a parsonage built at a total cost of $78,338. In the meantime, the Sanctuary was renovated. The

exterior underwent a process of pointing and washing which restored its original beauty. The interior ceiling was redecorated and the side walls replastered. The old parsonage which housed the pastors for years was moved to a new site and is being used for rental property.

Many members have been added to the church; the Sunday School reorganized, graded, and departmentalized and modern literature put into use—thus giving fresh impetus to the program of Religious Education. The Love Feast has been reinstituted and is being celebrated each Friday evening before the first Sunday. The spiritual life of the church has been awakened to a fuller consciousness of the meaning of Christianity by the fearless preaching of the gospel.

Rev. Johnston received his training at Dickerson Theological Seminary of Allen University and Atlanta University. On March 1, 1950, the degree of Doctor of Divinity was conferred upon him by Dickerson Theological Seminary. He began his career as a minister in May, 1927 and was ordained an elder November 16, 1934 by Bishop Noah W. Williams. His pastorates in North and South Carolina have been highly successful. In Sumter, South Carolina, June 10, 1943 Rev. Johnston and Miss Verdelle Ruth Jennings were happily married. They now have two daughters, Doris Marie and Loretta Ruth.

Mrs. Johnston is a graduate of South Carolina State College and a member of the Delta Sigma Theta Sorority. She is employed as an elementary teacher in the Durham City School System and is doing graduate work at North Carolina College at Durham in Special Education.

Mrs. Johnston successfully combines her career, household duties and church activities. In spite of the heavy demands upon her time and energy, there is always a warm welcome at the parsonage.

As citizens, Rev. and Mrs. Johnston have made a wonderful contribution to the city of

The Pastor's Family

Durham — which is strikingly evident to the passers-by. To this should be added their dynamic personalities, honesty, and sincerity of purpose— qualities which make them completely worthy of the best that life has to offer.

The Nursery School

Presiding Officers, Durham District

BISHOP L. H. HEMINGWAY,
D. D., LL.D
*Presiding Bishop, Second
Episcopal District*

REV. J. D. DAVIS, D. D.

Presiding Elder

REV. D. WILLIAMSON, D. D.

Former Presiding Elder

The Edian D. Markham Memorial Building

By act of the Official Board, March 17, 1952, the educational building was named the Edian D. Markham Memorial Building—a fitting tribute to the founder of St. Joseph Church. It further directed that a bronze plaque should be placed at some vantage spot in the building carrying the names of the Pastor, Rev. D. A. Johnston, and the trustees of the church.

Over the years, the membership has been accumulating funds for this project and during the administration of the late Rev. J. A. Valentine, the basement was completed to street level. We now have a modern parsonage and an educational building, adequately equipped with furniture which is both beautiful and enduring.

The physical structure has been completed and the spiritual structure is in course of development. In this connection, during the month of October, 1951, the following Board of Directors was named with Frank G. Burnett, Chairman, and Mrs. H. M. Michaux as Secretary. The first named persons are members of the Board and chairmen of their respective committees. *FINANCE*: G. W. Cox, J. H. Betts, Mrs. H. M. Michaux, J. J. Henderson, J. H. Wheeler, and N. H. Bennett; *FIRST AID*: Mrs. S. L. Dudley, Miss Pearl Henderson, Dr. J. N. Mills, and Dr. E. P. Norris; *NURSERY SCHOOL*: Mrs. C. F. Scarborough, F. D. Marshall, Mrs. S. V. Austin, Mrs. Pereppa Watkins; *MUSIC*: Mrs. Nell Hunter, Miss Andrea Burnett, T. R. Webber, Bennie

Lakin, Mrs. Lillian Buchanan, and Mrs. Hattie Scarborough; *A. C. E. LEAGUE*: Mrs. V. R. Johnston, Mrs. Mary Evans, and Mrs. Dorothy Manley; *GIRL SCOUTS*: Mrs. Josephine Strayhorn, Mrs. A. C. Lanier, Mrs. Beulah Hill, Mrs. C. Brown, and Miss A. L. Cobb; *BOY SCOUTS*: N. H. Bennett, Obadiah Barbee, Delaney Markham, L. W. Smith, and James I. Bolden; *RECREATION*: L. S. Gilliard; Mrs. W. M. Grandy, W. L. Cook, and H. M. Michaux, Jr.; *SOCIAL ACTIVITIES*: Mrs. M. C. Donnell, Miss A. M. Faulk, W. G. Rhodes, Mrs. J. H. Wheeler, and Miss Minnie Gilmer; *CHURCH HISTORY*: Rev. D. A. Johnston, Mrs. M. W. Amey, and Miss Evangelyn Vidal.

A Nursery School of St. Joseph A. M. E. Church has already been established, as of October 8, 1952, under the supervision of Miss Hattie Jenkins, assisted by Mrs. Maggie Guion and Mrs. Annie B. Brown. There are nine children in the first grade and thirty-four in the Nursery School, proper. The first grade is taught by Miss Jenkins and the Nursery School is in charge of Mrs. Guion. Wholesome meals are provided and proper rest periods observed. For convenience of the parents, the school opens at 7:45 A. M. and remains opened until the last child is called for. In order to render a real service to the community, the school will operate on a year-round plan.

This is simply a brief sketch of the Greater St. Joseph, for "it doth not yet appear what we shall be."

Program

Dedication of the Edian D. Markham Memorial Building and Parsonage

April 20-27, 1952

SUNDAY, APRIL 20

9:30 A. M.—SUNDAY SCHOOL .... W. G. Rhodes, *Superintendent*

11:00 A. M.—MORNING WORSHIP .... Message by the Pastor

3:00 P. M.—LAYMEN'S HOUR

      INTRODUCTION OF SPEAKER .... G. W. Cox

      GUEST SPEAKER .... Dr. C. C. Spaulding

                  President, North Carolina Mutual Life Insurance Company

                  Music by the Senior Choir

7:00 P. M.—EVENING WORSHIP .... Message by the Pastor

MONDAY, APRIL 21—8:00 P. M.

SERVICE BY COVENANT PRESBYTERIAN CHURCH .... Rev. J. A. Cannon, B. D., *Minister*

              Sponsored by Trustee and Steward Boards

TUESDAY, APRIL 22—8:00 P. M.

SERVICE BY FIRST CALVARY BAPTIST CHURCH ...., ... Rev. H. H. Hart, D. D., *Minister*

          Sponsored by Stewardess and Missionary Boards

WEDNESDAY, APRIL 23—8:00 P. M.

SERVICE BY MOREHEAD AVENUE BAPTIST CHURCH .... Rev. C. E. McLester, D. D., *Minister*

         Sponsored by the Class Leaders Council and Pastor's Aid Board

THURSDAY, APRIL 24—8:00 P. M.

SERVICE BY ST. MARK A. M. E. ZION CHURCH .... Rev. S. P. Perry, D. D., *Minister*

      Sponsored by the Ladies Aid Society, Satterfield-Davis Dramatic Club,

               and Daughters of St. Joseph

FRIDAY, APRIL 25—8:00 P. M.

SERVICE BY WEST DURHAM BAPTIST CHURCH . ... Rev. T. C. Graham, D. D., *Minister*

       Sponsored by the Sunday School, A C. E. League, and Usher Board

SUNDAY, APRIL 27

9:30 A. M.—SUNDAY SCHOOL .... W. G. Rhodes, *Superintendent*

11:00 A. M.—MORNING WORSHIP .... Message by Bishop L. H. Hemingway, D. D. LL, D.,

         Presiding Bishop of the Second Episcopal District, African Methodist Episcopal Church

3:00 P. M.—DEDICATORY SERVICE .... Bishop L. H. Hemingway

               and Presiding Elder J. D. Davis, Speakers

The Building Committee

Dedication of the Edian D. Markham Memorial Building

BISHOP: Dearly Beloved, by the favor of God and the labor of man, this building has been so far completed. It is to be a place where men and women, boys and girls may find opportunities for instruction, for recreation and ministries of fellowship.

Let us therefore bring to the Heavenly Father our praises for His guidance and aid in this undertaking, and our prayers on behalf of those who by their gifts or their service shall unite in fulfilling the purposes of love and good will for which this building is prepared.

MUSIC AND PRAYER

BISHOP: Wherefore David Blessed the Lord before all the congregation: and David said, "Blessed be Thou, Lord of Israel our Father, for ever and ever. Thine, O Lord, is the greatness, and the power, and the glory and the victory, and the majesty: for all that is in the heaven and in the earth is Thine; Thine is the kingdom, O Lord, and Thou are exalted as Head above all. Both riches and honor come of Thee, and Thou reigneth over all; and in Thine hand it is to make great, and to give strength unto all. Now, therefore, our God, we thank Thee, and praise Thy glorious Name. But who am I and what is my people, that we should be able to offer so willingly after this sort? For all things come of Thee, and of Thine own have we given Thee. For we are strangers before Thee, and sojourners, as were all our fathers: our days on the earth are as a shadow, and there is none abiding.

Our Lord our God, all this store that we have prepared to build Thee an house for Thine holy Name cometh of Thine hand, and is all Thine own. I know also, my God, that Thou triest the heart, and hast pleasure in uprightness. As for me, in the uprightness of mine heart I have willingly offered all these

things: and now have I seen with joy Thy people which are present here, to offer willingly unto Thee.

Though I speak with the tongues of men and of angels, and have not love, I am become as sounding brass or a tinkling cymbal. And though I have the gift of prophecy and understand all mysteries and all knowledge; and though I have all faith, so that I could remove mountains and have not love, I am nothing. And though I bestow all my goods to feed the poor, and though I give my body to be burned and have not love, it profiteth me nothing.

Love suffereth long, and is kind: love envieth not; love vaunteth not itself, is not puffed up, doth not behave itself unseemly, seeketh not her own is not easily provoked, thinketh no evil; rejoiceth not in iniquity, but rejoiceth in the truth; beareth all things, hopeth all things, endureth all things.

Love never faileth: but whether there be prophecies they shall fail; whether there be tongues they shall cease; whether there be knowledge it shall vanish away. For we know in part, and we prophesy in part. But when that which is perfect is come, then that which is in part shall be done away. When I was a child I spake as a child; I understood as a child, I thought as a child, but when I became a man I put away childish things. For now we see through a glass darkly; but then face to face: now I know in part; but then shall I know even as also I am known. And now abideth faith, hope, love, these three; but the greatest of these is love.

MUSIC

BISHOP: "I will give thanks unto the Lord with my whole heart."

PEOPLE: In the council of the upright, and in the congregation.

BISHOP: "The works of the Lord are great."

Berean Sunday School Class

PEOPLE: Sought out of all them that have pleasure therein.

BISHOP: "His work is honor and majesty."

PEOPLE: And his righteousness endureth forever.

BISHOP: "He hath made his wonderful works to be remembered."

PEOPLE: The Lord is gracious and merciful.

BISHOP: "He hath given food unto them that fear Him."

PEOPLE: He will ever be mindful of His covenant.

BISHOP: "He hath showed His people the power of His works."

PEOPLE: In giving them the heritage of the nations.

BISHOP: "The works of His hands are truth and justice."

PEOPLE: All His precepts are sure.

BISHOP: "They are established for ever and ever."

ALL: They are done in truth and uprightness.

GLORIA PATRIA: Glory be to the Father, and to the Son, and to the Holy Ghost: As it was in the beginning, is now, and ever shall be, world without end. Amen.

A TRUSTEE: We present unto you this building, to be dedicated to the service of Almighty God and the fellowship of His people.

BISHOP: Dearly beloved, it is right and proper that buildings erected for such service in the name of our Lord and Saviour Jesus Christ should be formally and devoutly set apart for their special uses. For such a dedication we are now assembled, and, as the dedication of this building is vain without the solemn consecration of these gifts and labors it represents, let us now give ourselves anew to the service of God: our souls that they may be renewed after the image of Christ; our bodies, that they may be fit temples for the indwelling of the Holy spirit; and our labors and business that they be according to God's holy will, and that their fruit may tend to the glory of God and the advancement of His kingdom.

PEOPLE STANDING AND RESPONDING

BISHOP: In the Name of the Father, and of the Son, and of the Holy Spirit, we dedicate this building as an educational building to the service of God and the uses of Christian fellowship.

PEOPLE: Whether therefore we eat or drink, or whatever ye do, do all to the glory of God.

BISHOP: We dedicate this building to the purpose of religious education: to the work of the Church School, to the study of the Scriptures, and to the development of Christian character.

PEOPLE: Whatsoever things are written aforetime were written for our learning; blessed are they that hear the words of God and keep it.

BISHOP: We dedicate this building to the broadening of mental horizons and the deepening of knowledge, that young and old may be awakened and informed.

PEOPLE: A man's wisdom maketh his face to shine, and the hardness of his face is changed.

BISHOP: We dedicate this building to those tasks and aims in which the Christian serves his place and time: to the cause of missions, of Christian citizenship, and the broad field of social relations.

PEOPLE: The kingdoms of this world are become the kingdoms of our Lord, and His Christ; and He shall reign for ever and ever.

BISHOP: We dedicate this building to Christian recreation of mind and body.

PEOPLE: Thou wilt show me the path of life; in Thy presence is fullness of joy; at Thy right hand there are pleasures for evermore.

ALL: We dedicate ourselves anew to that service of our fellowmen, wherein can best be performed our true service of God; in obedience to the spirit of the Master when He said: Thou shalt love the Lord thy God with all thy heart, and thy neighbor as thyself.

BISHOP: Let us pray. Almighty God, our Heavenly Father, whose eyes are ever toward the righteous, and whose ears are ever open unto their cry, graciously accept, we pray Thee, this building which we now

Dedication of Parsonage

"PEACE BE UNTO THIS HOUSE"

BISHOP: Dearly Beloved, members and friends of this household, it is written that, "Except the Lord build the house, they labor in vain that build it." We have therefore met here to invoke the divine blessing on this home, that its ties of love may be strong and beautiful through the blessing and the inspiration of the Heavenly Father.

MUSIC

BISHOP: "In the Name of the Father, and of the Son, and of the Holy Spirit, we dedicate this home to the glory of God, committing to His loving care this House and all who dwell in it."

PEOPLE: "Have thou respect unto the prayer of Thy servant O Lord my God which Thy servant prayeth before this day; that Thine eyes may be open toward this house night and day."

BISHOP: "We dedicate this home to the deep affection of the family circle, and to all friendly hospitalities."

Boy Scout Troop No. 105

Tour

Following the Dedication Ceremony, there will be a tour of the buildings. Guides: Mrs. Ruth Bolden, Miss Lucille Baines, Mrs. Jessie Moore, J. J. Henderson, Frank J. Burnett, J. H. Betts.

W. G. RHODES
Sunday School Superintendent

LEGACIES

Mrs. Carolina Bond (deceased) gave and bequeathed to St. Joseph A. M. E. Church seven (7) shares of American Tobacco Company preferred stock. From this source the church receives a quarterly contribution.

The late W. G. Pearson gave and devised to Saint Joseph A. M. E. Church a remainder interest in his home site at 806 Fayetteville Street, subject to the joint life estates of his neices, nephews, and other persons named in his will.

JAMES BAILEY
Oldest Living Member

REMEMBER?

During the lifetime of John Merrick, as an officer of St. Joseph, he always 'lifted" the collection. In making his appeal for an offering, he often jovially admonished the congregation by saying, "Brothers and Sisters, if you don't put some money on this table today, we'll just have to stop doing business here on this spot."

D. J. JAMES
Caretaker, Steward and Class Leader

MISS LUCILLE BAINES
Church Secretary

MRS. NELL HUNTER
Director, Senior Choir

*Steward
Board*

*Stewardess
Board No. 2*

Moxahalia Sunday School Class

day

Gospel
Choir

Usher
Board

Above: Congregation, March 12, 1951 ; Below: Sunday School, March 12, 1951

Pastor's Aid Board

Bessie Amey Mills Sunday School Class

Historical Data: African Methodist Episcopal Church And Its Founder

Richard Allen

American Negro Clergyman, was born of slave parents in Philadelphia, Pa., in 1760. Soon after his birth his parents were sold into slavery in Delaware. At 17 years of age he joined the Methodist Episcopal Church and when 22 years old was licensed to preach. Four years later (1786) he purchased his freedom for $2,000, Continental money and returned to Philadelphia. Here he joined St. George's M. E. Church in which he was permitted to preach to colored people at five o'clock meetings. Dissatisfied with the restrictions placed upon those who attended these meetings, he decided to withdraw. He personally purchased a lot at the corner of Sixth and Lombard

RICHARD ALLEN   SARAH ALLEN

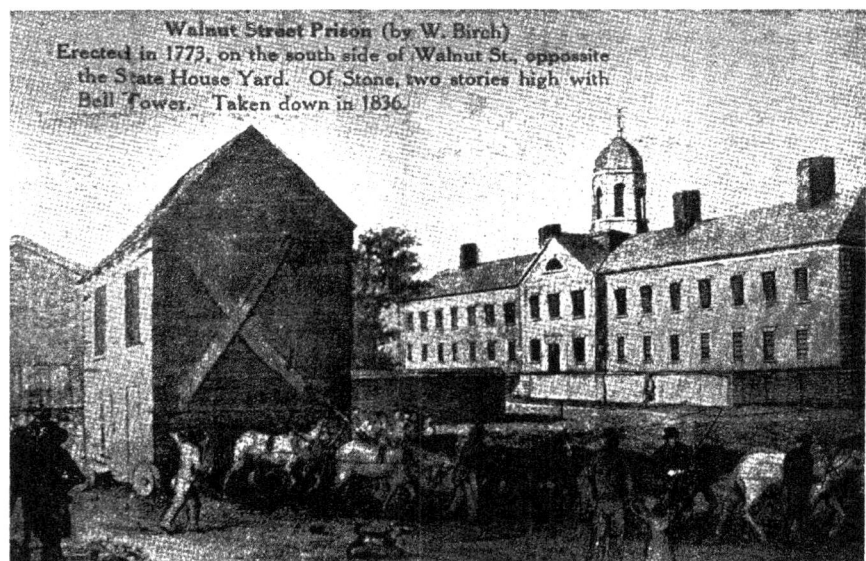

The moving of the blacksmith shop from Eighth and Walnut to Sixth Street below Pine, which later became the first church of African Methodism known as the Blacksmith Shop Meeting House. Richard Allen was a teamster by trade. In the picture you can see him with his team hauling the blacksmith shop.

Streets, and moved upon it an old blacksmith snop which he refurnished as a house of worship. Here he organized in 1787 the first church for colored people in the United States. His followers who congregated here were called Allenites. Despite opposition and a series of obstructive lawsuits, a charter was secured from the General Assembly of Pennsylvania. A new church building was erected and opened in 1794. It was dedicated by Bishop Francis Asbury and called *Bethel*. In 1799 Allen was regularly ordained in the ministry of the Methodist Episcopal Church, the first colored minister so ordained. In 1816, upon the organization of the African Methodist Episcopal Church, Allen was elected bishop. He died in Philadelphia on March 26, 1831.

Encyclopedia Britannica

------:------

Richard Allen's Ideals

(1) A church connection which knows no color barrier. (2) A church connection which bases its concept upon the equality of man and human decency. (3) A church connection which fosters educational leadership for the Negro people. (4) A church connection which has not strayed from the original concept and teachings of Jesus.

Dr. Helen G. Edmonds, Professor of History, NCC at Durham, "History-African Methodism."

------:------

Q. By whom was it (African Methodist Episcopal Church) organized?

A. Rev. Richard Allen and fifteen others.

Q. Give the names of the other fifteen.

A. Jacob Tapisco, Clayton Durham, James Champion, and Thomas Webster of Philadelphia; Daniel Coker, Richard Williams, Henry Harden, Stephen Hill, Edward Williamson and Richard Gailliard of Baltimore, Maryland; Peter Spencer of Wilmington, Delaware; Jacob Marsh, Edward Jackson, and William Andrews of Attleborough, Pennsylvania; and Reuben Cuff, Salem, New Jersey.

Methodist Polity— Bishop H. M. Turner

------:------

Church Motto

God our Father, Christ our Redeemer, and Man our Brother.

------:------

Q. What is a sacrament?

A. A sacred ordinance enjoined by Christ, the Head of the Christian Church, to be observed by his followers, and which binds us to him anew —rebinding.

Q. How many sacraments are there?

A. Two: Baptism and Lord's Supper.

Methodist Polity— Bishop H. M. Turner

------:------

. . . . as early as 1778, in the city where the Constitution of the United States was struck off, we

The *Second Church of African Methodism.* This *church is known as a rough-cast church.*

The *Third Church was made of red brick.* This *church was the scene of the first General Conference in 1816 where Richard Allen was made the first bishop and served as pastor of the church and also as bishop until his death.*

see through the sources the first organization approximating the nature of a combination against risk incidental to sickness and death. Here under the designation of "The Free African Society" was probably the first manifestation of independent economic cooperation among Negroes. There is something worthy, in more than the ordinary sense, about the efforts of this small group of isolated folk to look after their sick, care for their poor, and bury their dead. The leaders of this organization were persons of prominence. Among the charter members were *Richard Allen*, the founder of the African Methodist Episcopal Church, and Absalom Jones, the most distinguished Negro preacher of the Episcopal Church at that time.

The Journal of Negro History, October, 1937.

Recent Tributes Paid To Richard Allen

A housing project in the city of Philadelphia is known as the "Richard Allen Homes."

In 1949, the city of Philadelphia set aside a day known as "Richard Allen Day." The following is the proclamation issued by the Mayor of that city:

WHEREAS, Richard Allen, founder and first Bishop of the African Methodist Episcopal Church, was born a slave in Philadelphia and subsequently purchased his freedom by hard work and the rendering of useful service, and

WHEREAS, despite the lack of formal training Allen, during the yellow fever plague which raged in the city in 1793 killing thousands of people, risked his own life and saved hundred of the stricken victims, and

WHEREAS, his people were held in physical bondage totally unlettered and had no opportunity for education, Richard Allen established day and night schools which gave training to the victims of the slave system, and

WHEREAS, when the British Army occupied Washington, the Capital of the Nation, and seriously threatened Philadelphia, Allen organized twenty-five hundred men who became known as the "Black Legion" to defend the city. Allen was a great patriot, contemporary with Benjamin Franklin, Dr. Benjamin Rush, George Washington and other great leaders of the Revolutionary period, and

WHEREAS, Richard Allen established and maintained a station of the underground railroad which gave assistance and hope to the slave striving for freedom,

NOW, THEREFORE I, Bernard Samuel, Mayor of the City of Philadelphia, do hereby declare Thursday, June 30, 1949 as RICHARD ALLEN DAY.

Given under my hand and the Seal of the City of Philadelphia this twenty-third day of June, one thousand nine hundred forty-nine.

———:———

RICHARD ALLEN was a man of independent character as shown by his conception of religion, by his unwillingness to have others support him, by his unwillingness to travel as a preacher's assistant in the South and sleep in his carriage at night, by his resentment of the treatment of his people at St. George. He was a thrifty man. As a slave he did more work than other slaves; he always could find work; he seemed to have a good trader; he owned several teams when Bethel was established though he had been in Philadelphia but a short while. He was a man of integrity. Even as a slave when he delivered a message, his word was taken and he did not have to bear a note with his master's signature. When the first property was purchased for the African Church though a majority of the committee wanted to give up the property and did so, Allen had given his word, and therefore kept it. And this should always be remembered in connection with the oldest piece of property owned by any Negro organization in the country — the first bond on it was Richard Allen's word.

Encyclopedia of African Methodism

"Mother Bethel" A. M. E. Church, built by the late Bishop Cornelius T. Schaffer. The blacksmith shop was the first church on this site. There were four other buildings. Richard Allen's tomb is in the basement. A historical room contains a number of relics. The plot on which this church is built is probably the oldest piece of real estate owned by any Negro organization.

———:———

1827—"Daughters of the Conference" organized—first woman's conference society.

—:—

1837—First A. M. E. Church organized in New England, at New Haven, Conn.

—:—

1842—Notable year for church building, Mother Bethel being completed at a cost of $18,000.

—:—

1846—The New York Conference passes first resolution for Preachers Aid Society.

—:—

1848—New Bethel, Baltimore, dedicated, costing $16.000.

—:—

1856—The British A. M. E. Church organized, at Chatham, Ontario, September 27, and Bishop Nazery elected its head.

—:—

1865—Bishop Payne organized, May 15, the South Carolina Conference, which then embraced all of the southeastern part of the United States.

Encyclopedia of African Methodism

Statistical Data, Year Ending 1950-1951

Number of local churches	5,878
Total membership	1,166,301
Number of Sunday School teachers and officers	38,832
Number of Pastors having charges	5,878
Total number of ordained men	7,089
Number of women pastors having charges	45
Total number of ordained women	84

Bureau of History and Research, Bishop Reverdy C. Ransom, Director

———:———

No discussion of the African Methodist Episcopal Church is complete without due recognition being given to its pioneer efforts in the various fields of endeavor.

In 1844, plans were laid for the first A. M. E. School—a manual labor school near Columbus, Ohio. In 1855 Wilberforce University was established by the Methodist Church with the A. M. E. Church cooperating. In 1863, Bishop Daniel A. Payne bought Wilberforce University, now the oldest and one of the largest Negro institutions of higher learning in America. Since then an institution of learning has been established by the church in nearly every state in the South: Allen University, Columbia, South Carolina; Morris Brown College, Atlanta, Georgia; Edward Waters College, Jacksonville, Florida; Daniel Payne College, Birmingham, Alabama; Campbell College, Jackson, Mississippi; Paul Quinn College, Waco, Texas; Shorter College, Little Rock,

SHORTER HALL, WILBERFORCE UNIVERSITY. Built in the nineteen-twenties at a cost of $271,-000. Houses classrooms, administrative offices and auditorium with seating capacity of 1600, and three floors of dormitory space.

Arkansas; Kittrell College, Kittrell, North Carolina; Western University, Quindaro, Kansas. There are several high schools and elementary schools, both in America and in foreign countries. All of these institutions, except Wilberforce University, Western University, and Kittrell College are named for some of the earlier bishops of the church. In each of these colleges is a theological school for the training of ministers.

The A. M. E. school property is valued at more than $6,000,000. The cultural influence

DUKE MEMORIAL HALL, KITTRELL COLLEGE, the third oldest college owned and controlled by the A. M. E. Church.

GOMEZ ADMINISTRATION BUILDING, PAUL QUINN COLLEGE'S new administration building, valued at $150,000, is almost completed, with dedication set for April 29. The Austin stone structure is completely fireproof, and will house six classrooms, bookstore, post office, directors' room, burglar-proof vaults, and all of the administrative offices of the college and the Tenth District of the African Methodist Episcopal Church under whose auspices the college is operated.

wielded by these institutions cannot be estimated in dollars and cents, for in the towns and cities of the U. S. A. and elsewhere can be found men and women who bear the earmarks of the training received in the Christian atmosphere of these halls of learning.

. The A. M. E. Church pioneered in journalism. The "Christian Recorder," published in Philadelphia is the oldest weekly published by Negroes in the world — 105 years to be exact. "The A. M. E. Review" is 68 years old, the oldest Negro magazine in the world. The A. M. E. Book Concern," the oldest weekly publishing business in the world for Negroes, is 136 years old and has been incorporated 97 years. The pioneer work in writing and printing Sunday School commentaries was done for Negroes by the Sunday School Union, started 65 years ago.

The first Negro missionaries sent by Negroes to Africa were sent by the A. M. E. Church whose Missionary Department is over 100 years old. It sent a missionary to Haiti in 1826, to Africa in 1887. Bishop H. M. Turner was the pioneer African bishop having gone to West Africa in 1891 and South Africa in 1898. In these two sections of Africa we now have over 100,000 members and three episcopal districts.

The Discipline of the A. M. E. Church is the oldest book of law published by Negroes in the United States of America and the A. M. E. Hymnal is the first book of hymns to be printed by Negroes.

Today the African Methodist Episcopal Church has a million members scattered all over America, as well as West, Central and South Africa, South America, Canada, Mexico, and the West Indies. In no part of the world is the church growing more rapidly than in South Africa, where we have Wilberforce Institute, an accredited teacher training college; The R. R. Wright, Jr. School of Religion for training ministers; Bethel Institute at Capetown; and scores of elementary schools with a total enrollment of over 15,000. The A. M. E.'s furnished the first Negro college president and the first German Ph. D.

Our main job is to bring people to the knowledge of God and to bring Negroes to the understanding that they too are children of God . . . and to persuade America and the world to practice the principles of the Christian religion.

Encyclopedia of African Methodism

IN CONCLUSION

During the 165 years of African Methodism, many generations have played their parts and passed off the stage. We, in our time, are making history for our great church. When future generations shall review our achievements, may each of us say to them, in spirit, that * "With the days that I had and the strength that I had, I have done what I could toward that progress. When the pyramid is finished, my grain of sand will be part of it."

* Channing Pollock—"*Adventures of a Happy Man*" By permission of his daughter, Miss Helen Pollock.

Congratulations To St. Joseph A. M. E. Church

On Its New Educational Building

LET US SERVE YOU

DURHAM DISTRICT OFFICE
NORTH CAROLINA MUTUAL LIFE INSURANCE CO.
606½ FAYETTEVILLE STREET

C. C. SPAULDING, *President*   W. L. COOKE, *District. Manager*

C. C. SMITH, JR., *Assistant Manager*
L. Z. CRAFT, *Assistant Manager*
N. L. DONAGHUE, *Assistant Manager*
MRS. M. W. HAMLETT, *Cashier*
MRS. J. A. PRATT, *Secretary*
MRS. JANET M. MARCHENA, *Assistant Cashier*

SPECIAL ORDINARY

C. M. PALMER
C. R. RIVERS
J. L. LASSITER

REPRESENTATIVES	*REPRESENTATIVES*
• ALEXANDER U. ARRINGTON	• PAUL McALLISTER
• MRS. LESSIE BATTLE	• JAMES MADKINS
• W. W. BARBEE	• T. T. MORSE
• GEORGE BOOKER	• VERNON PARKER
• RAYMOND FREEMAN	• LAWRENCE PERRY
• HENRY GARNER	• JAMES L. ROGERS
• SAMUEL HARRIS	• W. E. STUBBS
• MRS. EFFIE JONES	• CHARLIE TORAIN
• FREDDIE J. JOHNSON	• IRA WALKER
• JAMES LLOYD	• ANDREW WALLACE
• T. EARL LAMBETH	• CHARLES WILLIAMS

"No Home Complete Without North Carolina Mutual Policies"

Lightning Source UK Ltd.
Milton Keynes UK
UKHW020632060119
334855UK00006B/170/P

9 780265 581377